Ideas and Inspirations
Abstract Quilts in Solids

...a book for grown-up quilters

Quilt Design and Author
© 2008, Gwen Marston
(231) 448-2565 | www.gwenmarston.com
Beaver Island, Michigan, USA

Photography and Book Design
© 2008, gregory case photography
(408) 248-9721 | photos@gregorycase.com | www. gregorycase.com
Sunnyvale, California, USA

Front cover: *Mexican Hat Dance*. 40" X 47", 2008. Hand Quilted.
Inside cover: *Checkerboard Medallion*. 27" x 32", 2008. Hand Quilted.
Back cover: *High Desert Country III*. 34" X 36", 2008. Hand Quilted.

The main font used in this book is Galliard. All other text, including chapter titles, headings, and sub-headings is in Syntax.

All rights to this publication and its contents are reserved. No part of this book may be reproduced, stored in an information retrieval system, or transcribed in any form by any means, graphic, electronic, or mechanical — without the prior written permission by the publisher, MoCa Press.

ISBN 978-0-6152-4581-2
First Edition/August 2008

MoCa Press • San Jose, CA • Printed in the USA by Lulu.com

Additional copies of this book are available through Gwen Marston (author), gregory case (photographer), selected bookstores, and through www.Lulu.com. You can also purchase a PDF version (e-book) through www.Lulu.com.

Ideas and Inspirations
Abstract Quilts in Solids

Quilts and Text
by Gwen Marston

Photography
by gregory case

...a book for grown-up quilters

MoCa Press • San Jose, CA

Ideas and Inspirations
Abstract Quilts in Solids

About this book

This is a book for grownup quilters. It's a book for the many accomplished quilters who are not looking for yet another project book with pages of detailed elementary instructions on how to make someone else's quilt. Rather, it's intended for quilters who are seeking ideas and inspiration for their own work. In my quilt related travels, I've had the pleasure of meeting many such veteran quilters.

This book was also developed to help celebrate the 25th anniversary of my Beaver Island Quilt Retreats (BIQR). Quilters who come to these retreats come with the expectation that they will be provided with an abundance of ideas which will help them design their own original work. The new works in this book were made specifically to provide ideas and inspiration to support the 2008 BIQR theme of making abstract quilts in solids.

About these quilts

The first quilts I made with solids were quilts made in the Amish style in an effort to understand those quilts and the Amish use of color. Since that beginning, I have continued to use solids in my work including liberated, abstract work. "Liberated quiltmaking" is a phrase I coined in 1990 to describe new improvisational methods of making quilts that involved free piecing rather than using templates. Eight quilts in the book were made prior to 2007 with the remainder made since then. My intent with this recent work with solids was to simplify the elements, to melt them down to their most basic forms and thus to allow the color to speak in a stronger voice. All quilts are machine sewn, two are tied, and the others are hand quilted.

Working with solids

Quilts made in solids have an impressive history. Quilts stitched in solids were the first quilts to be taken seriously as art. In 1971, Amish quilts from the collection of Jonathan Holstein and Gail van der Hoof constituted the first major museum exhibition of quilts shown at the Whitney Museum of American Art in New York. At the time, it caused as much of a sensation as did the quilts from Gee's Bend shown more recently in museums around the country.

Solids and prints both have their own particular advantages and both bring certain unique design qualities to the table. In my own work, I have dipped into these two paint pots with equal enthusiasm.

Here are a few qualities inherent in solids.

- Solids seem more painterly than printed fabrics if for no other reason than that paint itself comes in solids, not prints. For example, paint does come in pastels, but not in "Aunt Gracie's reproduction prints."

- Line and form are more clearly defined in quilts made with solids. Solids emphasize more clearly the delineation between shapes whereas prints can blur the edges of adjoining shapes.

- Prints bring with them a specific character. Some prints evoke whole story lines. When working with solids you have to create character.

- Prints contain pattern. When working with solids you have to create pattern if you want pattern.

- Hand quilting shows up best on solids and thus offers opportunities to dramatically enhance a quilt. Quilting lines add a secondary design element, which play a major role in the look of the work. Because the stitching lines are clearly seen, they can be used to reinforce the design elements or to create patterns where none existed. The distinctive appearance of hand quilting adds a soft classical texture long associated with quilts and one that continues to have great appeal.

- Quilts made with solids are harder to date than quilts made with prints and are therefore, less likely to appear "dated."
- Solids have no right or wrong side to the fabric so while this fact doesn't contribute in an artistic way, it does contribute to technical ease.

I have always been drawn to quilts with bold graphic design and find working with solids gives me results I like. My love affair with solids began early and continues to this day. While this is the first time I've addressed this subject in book form, there are quilts made of solids in all my previous books.

Design and construction

"Do you have a degree in art?"
"No, but I lived in Kansas when I was young."

This is an exchange I have frequently, perhaps because the classes I teach focus on design. Living on the prairie as I did long ago, I found with less to see, I learned to look more carefully. Actually, it's not that there is less to see in Kansas, it's just that it isn't as dramatic as mountains or waterfalls, so you have to take time and *really* look. I can remember like it was yesterday, riding my horse along country roads in the winter and concentrating on discovering the very many shades of brown along the sides of the road and as far as the eye could see. My point is that while I do not have a degree in art, I learned early the value of careful observation, I've practiced it ever since, and I think it's a critical skill for an artist to have. I taught myself how to "see."

The greatest inspiration for my work has been antique quilts. I look at all the elements that make up a quilt and how they relate to each other to create the overall effect. I study quilts in detail: the colors, the individual blocks, the format, the border, and the quilting.

The quilts in this book were constructed using a method I call "liberated" which I explored in depth in *Liberated Quiltmaking* (AQS, 1996). It's a way of working that is intuitive and improvisational. The thesaurus provides optional words, which remind us of what "improvisational" means: making do, inventiveness, ad-libbing, making it up as you go along, extemporization, winging it. It is not overly studied. I find I'm far more likely to make a break-through and create successful work if I take some chances.

I begin with a seed of an idea, plant it, and let it grow. I make the design decisions as the quilt is being made. It's like making chili: you begin with the main ingredients and add seasoning to taste. The "main ingredients" include the form I'm going to use as building blocks (such as Liberated Log Cabin), the prominent colors to be used, the scale, and the complexity of the elements. The "seasonings" are the way I spice up my work by adding accent colors, a bit of a printed fabric, or a textured fabric.

One of my favorite building blocks for abstract work is the Liberated Log Cabin, which begins with a center and builds outward in an unstructured way. I like this form because of its endless options. As I make each block, I think of it as a single composition. They can be complex or simple. They can include many angles, or few angles. They can be made with large pieces or small pieces. They can be squared to the same size and sewn into rows. Or they can be squared to the same height, but allowed to remain different in width, and joined into rows.

As with everything else in life, the hardest part is getting started. I find that once I get started, the ideas begin to flow. Once you get started, the quilt will begin to lead the way and ideas will come to you. Often I feel as though the quilt is making itself and I'm the facilitator.

Making quilts can be an adventuresome journey when you don't have a roadmap. It's rather like taking a trip in a snowstorm: you can only see a few feet in front of you but you can make the whole trip that way.

How to use the ideas in this book to inspire your own work

This book shows full page photographs of all the quilts in true color. Having high quality photographs large enough so you can actually see what is going on means that grownup quilters like you can clearly see how the quilts are constructed. Detailed close-ups and the captions provide additional construction clues and information. These quilts were either made in small units or in long strips, which were then sewn together to complete the top. If you follow the seam lines, you can see how the quilt was constructed.

Lastly, in *The Old Way of Seeing: How Architecture Lost its Magic and How to Get it Back,* Jonathan Hale says, "Intellect has its place but we do not know when to stop analyzing." I don't think you have to suffer through endless planning and analysis to make a good quilt. I invite you to just get started and enjoy the process.

Medallion
54" X 54"
2007
Hand Quilted
[1]

The medallion format makes a great canvas for laying down lively color. A sophisticated black print joins the mix adding a subtle accent. This quilt is a relative of the last quilt in the book, Wool Medallion [27].

Strippy
39" X 49"
2007
Hand Quilted
[2]

Strippy quilts have their origin in the British Isles. They are a traditional format quilters have long used to organize unruly scraps.

Liberated Log Cabin
38" X 46"
2007
Hand Quilted
[3]

This quilt directly inspired Red Square II [4], which in turn led to Red Square III [5].

Red Square II
39" X 42"
2007
Hand Quilted
[4]

I used the red square framed in gold from Liberated Log Cabin [3] as the central theme to create this quilt.

Red Square III
43" X 45"
2007
Hand Quilted
[5]

This quilt uses the idea of the little framed square from Red Square II [4] in a repeated pattern. Here is a very simple idea, the "less is more" concept in action.

Liberated Log Cabin in Neutrals, Blacks and Reds
44" X 65"
2007
Hand Quilted
[6]

This quilt was made with larger blocks, a scrappy pieced border and a black print stirred into the mix.

Medallion with Sawtooth Border
40" X 43"
2008
Hand Quilted
[7]

The definition of a medallion quilt is a quilt that begins with an area of interest surrounded by various borders. This is a liberated version of the classic medallion.

Broken Dishes
37" X 38"
2008
Hand Quilted
[8]

This is one of a number of quilts I've constructed with the idea of building one large Liberated Log Cabin block.

Red Square VI
39" X 42"
2008
Hand Quilted
[9]

This is another experiment with red squares. This time they are dancing about on a neutral background.

Framed Red Squares
40" X 44"
2007
Hand Quilted
[10]

Here I present the red square arranged in an orderly fashion with just a few changes in the size of the elements.

Liberated Log Cabin with Black Slivers
39 ½" X 44"
2008
Hand Quilted
[11]

My recipe for this quilt was to use clear colors, relatively simple blocks, and thin black lines as accents.

High Desert Country
34" X 36 ½"
2007
Hand Quilted
[12]

On a fall drive from Portland to Sisters, Oregon, I was overwhelmed with the colors of that exquisite high desert country.

High Desert Country II
34" X 34"
2007
Hand Quilted
[13]

This is the second quilt made using colors borrowed from the high desert landscape around Sisters, Oregon.

High Desert Country III
34" x 36"
2008
Hand Quilted
[14]

This is a third in the series of quilts inspired by the high desert country.

String Strippy
41" X 49"
2008
Hand Quilted
[15]

I think of String quilts as the "Jackson Pollack's" of the quilt world. Improvisation is the very soul of the string quilt.

Triangles
46" X 46"
2008
Hand Quilted
[16]

This quilt relies on a simple repeated shape in a classic setting for a clean, effective look. By letting the triangles turn in different directions they form new shapes.

A Few Red Squares
45" X 55"
2008
Hand Quilted
[17]

This quilt began life as a traditional Square Within a Square and then changed its predictable course with the addition of a few red squares.

Liberated Log Cabin With Appliquéd Borders
36" X 36"
2008
Hand Quilted
[18]

This quilt was an effort to work in soft colors and simple forms. I credit an antique quilt with the idea of the double continuous vine border.

Liberated Log Cabin with Purple Border
58" X 73"
2000
Hand Quilted
[19]

Pieced with discarded scraps from other projects, these blocks vary in width so they don't line up and thus create a more complex overall design.

Wedges and Slivers
31" X 37 ½"
2006
Hand Quilted
[20]

This quilt could be called a liberated rail fence, or just as easily, a basic string quilt.

Cut-Out Corners with Square Within a Square Borders
45" X 45"
2005
Hand Quilted
[21]

The design of this quilt was inspired by a New England linsey-woolsey quilt c.1820. The quilting designs are based on the large floral motifs common in 16th century bed rugs.

Summer Fruit Salad
44" X 51"
2001
Hand Quilted
[22]

Making a fairly large number of Liberated Log Cabin quilts, I always begin with a new recipe. Here, the idea was two-fold: working with solids in summer fruit salad colors and working small. These blocks finish 3".

Liberated Log Cabin with Brown Border
42" X 49"
2000
Hand Quilted
[23]

Quilts in this style were made by Americans from all backgrounds including the Amish. Made of solids, their quilts were magnificent which didn't go unnoticed in my house.

Tied Log Cabin
28" X 32"
1997
Tied
[24]

I bought these fabrics in Japan intrigued with the idea of using textured fabrics to add subtle interest.

Liberated Square Within a Square
42" X 46"
1996
Hand Quilted
[25]

Here is a simple traditional block in its liberated form pieced with home dyed fabrics.

Mexican Hat Dance
40" X 47"
2008
Hand Quilted
[26]

Made with one repeated, liberated unit in hot colors, this quilt seems to fairly dance, hence the name.

Wool Medallion
18 ½" X 18 ½"
1988
Tied
[27]

I thought this was a good quilt in 1988 and I still think it is, so much so that I elaborated on the idea with the Medallion quilt [1].